*To every open heart that needs a sign of guidance from God!*

# Visions of My Heart

## Kayla Ross

Fulton Books, Inc.
Meadville, PA

Published by Fulton Books 2022

ISBN 979-8-88731-248-4 (paperback)
ISBN 979-8-88731-247-7 (digital)

Printed in the United States of America

# Contents

# A Prayer for My Readers!

Lord, in the name of Jesus, bless their soul and open their eyes like you did Saul of Tarsus. Turn them into Paul where their eyes and ears are open. To every victory, they are righteous. They are children of the highest God. Lord, they are reading this book for a reason. Lord, bless their health, faith, and relationships. Give them the strength of Samson to fight the good fight of faith. Lord, hold them when their weak and enter into their storm. The woman or man who is reading this book, bless them with the favor of man. I decree and declare Psalm 91 over their lives. Whatever you have blessed will not and cannot be cursed. Cleanse their souls and hearts to see the golden light of Christ Jesus. Give them strength in being a mother, father, son, daughter, husband, or wife. In Jesus's name, they are completely forgiven by you, Father (Col. 1:14). Lord, let them get personal with you, Father, and because they picked up this book, bless them. Father, in your holy name (Eph. 3:12), in Jesus's name, amen.

# Introduction

I am Kayla Ross, a fifteen-year-old writer, the author of this book. What inspired me to write this book was to spread light and wisdom to all generations. This book is a book of poems to share with you the inner me—the visions that inspire me and also the truth that builds me as a young lady. This book is titled *Visions of My Heart*. These poems show dreams, visions, and experiences that I have had; some are based on true stories in my life. Off the dreams, I want to become reality. I really wanted to inspire my generation. I want them to see a young face on the cover of a book that they would want to pick it up and read about. I also have a message behind each poem that conveys wisdom. I learned that wisdom does not come through age but through experience. Faith is powerful to me, and this book is not just for Christians but also for the faint of heart. Therefore, I encourage you to read and think of the messages being conveyed. Learn the depth of the message and its story and the appreciation of the things and people around you that simply create you. Thank you so much for buying this book. I hope you genuinely enjoy it and learn something from it. I also pray that it will bless every area of your life! Thank you!

# I Will Be

I will be a strong, independent, and intelligent Black woman.
I will be a dancer of many styles and leader to the young.
I will be the wisdom of my elders for their words I speak.
I will be a writer of many poems and strong wise mother to my
  children.
I will be a songwriter where music flows through my lips. Words of
  faith, love, and hope reach through my hands through my pen
  to my paper.
I will be strong in the knowledge of God; through my eyes, I see a
  vision God has laid before me.
Faith is the one thing I can depend on.
Through my eyes, with Jesus on my side, I look and see the reward
  of the righteous.
I will be roaming the world traveling to new destinations. But never
  forgetting my foundation.
For one place I cannot choose, few see the dreams I want to accom-
  plish. Although man's eyes are little, my eyes are wide open to
  the goals I will achieve.
Man wants me to write a poem of the words he has given me about
  travel, fun, and things that will be.
However, God directed me to greater.
You might not know my name, but you will know me by the fruit I
  bear.
A girl who has turned into a woman.
With many talents that God sent from heaven above.
I will be me, Kayla Ross.

# *Time*

Time is short but time is long.
Time is small but time is wide.
Few take it for granted; some waste it on problems which they cannot control.
Few places I have been, but the ocean I have not seen.
The water I did not feel; it flows as time flows like a stream.
I sit in my chair and rock to flashes in time.
My eyes opened or closed time flows like a river.
I remember that past when I was an innocent baby.
I dream of the future young and old.
For that time is none.
Time, why does it go for another child to be born in the cold?
If I could go back to that memory, I would.
Oh yes, time can be evil or good.
Fast or slow, but when time hits, what will you do?

# Tunnel Vision

I saw the light at the end of the tunnel.
I held it and ran it was a tunnel vision.
Something seen but undone.
Vision can be spiritual or natural.
All things are not seen through your natural eyes.
For what is a dream.
Flowers grow; a tree stands.
The sun shines that I see.
My mind, my flesh says flowers die; love grows old.
Wow, which vision do I choose?
A vision of love or a paintball of untruth thrown in my face.
Tunnel vision is truth.

# *Lion*

A lion attacks his prey.
But without his pride, he is weak.
For a selfish lion cannot eat.
He cries a sweet lullaby.
For everyone needs help, even a tree.
And when that lion roars, a pain release.
A male Simba walks by and says, "Son,
Be strong. Come to the pride, for we are one."
The lion grabs the dirt.
His paw meets the river.
He stares at the water.
To see what God has delivered.
With every stride, he walks with a growl; he smiles.
For his pride, he found waiting at a den.
He is not alone.
He is welcomed home.

# Body

I look inside me, I see my veins, I see flaws.
I look at my heart, I see a reward.
I look at my lungs, I see oxygen.
I look at my blood; I see Christ on the cross.
I look at the outside body to see my skin.
I look at my legs running to victory.
I look at my hands; I see a pen and an angel who flies by.
I look at my arms and see me boxing for my independence.
The body is powerful; the mind is great for 10 percent.
But who pushes the body?

# Ocean

A bird is small, but the sky is an infant.
The ocean is enormous; a mighty whale fits inside.
A human is a small molecule who swims on its shores.
There is the beginning, middle, and end.
Some live in the deep bottom where it is dark.
Few tiny lights you can find.
Behold the unseen, complex, filled, and disciplined.
Salty drying your mouth out like dust.
A boat is needed to float above the surface.
The ocean what an incredible place.
You can see the horizon of the sun.
Raising or falling beyond the ocean into the tides.

# Rich Man

I wait at the riverbank waiting to see the awake.
I sit in plain but unseen sight.
As demons prowl and angels fight.
I am rich I gain the world.
The fool man falls into a swirl.
A rich man can be treacherous in his despise.
Therefore, at the feud, he awakes.
When will the poor man rise?
Money is good; so is peace.
When I sit and encounter this rain.
Which one do I prefer money or peace?
For in a feud and in drama comes a great deal of money.

# The Little Lost Girl

Girl born into sin, with a mother thick and thin, thin line between
love and hate.
When her father is awake, she opens her eyes to an earthquake.
Takes her first breath, she hides between doom and shame.
Parents let their child be doomed to their fate.
At five, she cried, sorrow awakes.
At ten, she is raped; from love, she lost faith.
Little does she know love can be great.
At fourteen, she is lost.
Her father was her lost protector.
Her family was her lost shield; she grew up poor.
Eighteen she was grown, poor, busted, and disgusted.
What did she feel as her soul escaped?
She found truth at twenty.
A little lost girl was her foundation.
She looks up at the sky; she looks down at the ground.
To kneel to say demons exist, she looks up and screams, "Why?"
Walks down a road and a little boy says, "My little sister, Jesus will
fight."
She takes four steps one to let go.
Two to forgive her enemies.
Three to forgive herself.
Four to run and meet Jesus at the light.
She found a light that shined so bright a fire that burned her from
the inside.
Cleanse her heart and made it white again Jesus held her hand.

# Love

Love is just a simple word.
Few use this term in a family or with friends.
But this word is powerful thick not thin.
Why do humans desire this feeling if it is just an element?
Love can make a poor man or even a rich man happy.
Love fills the heart with a sprinkle of dust.
Like the tooth fairy when she comes to lay a dollar under your pillow.
I reckon the sun shines in December when love enters the winter.
Love brings peace.
Can also make you fight for what you believe.
Love brings joy and laughter that fills your soul.
Love fills the emptiness and the hunger inside.
Love keeps a marriage going forever.
Love makes a mother hold her child.
Fight to protect and guard her child.
Love makes a father go to work.
Love makes life seem a little less complex.
Love creates a bond a relationship with anyone.
Love is not confusion or lost in tragedy.
Love quite the memory.
Love is looking beyond.
Love does not die it goes on.

# Water

Water is just a beautiful feature. Everyone needs its embrace; fun,
    laughter, jokes, and cries come with water.
Water can bring someone back to health.
A simple flower needs water a drop maybe two.
Water is clear, but molecules fit inside.
That salty water that drops from our eyes.
The clouds rain as if they cry with such disgrace.
For when it rains, there is gloom, but soon comes harvest and crops.
Even a tornado needs rain pulls up the things that rain helped create.
What movement creates the rain?
It is just a simple element in time of Earth's thick and thine.
Can't water be made into wine?

# Flower

Colorful little, tiny thing that starts as a tiny seed.
Water and sun bring a beam of life to that little sweet thing.
Bee's love it as if it were a woman with beautiful hair as its leaves.
That bee creates honey how sweet.
Let's say that bee is pretty sprung off that pollen.
For him, a relief to look around at the field of life surrounded by
     nature.
And its might, flower purple, red and white.
The smell of the roses.
They hum a sweet tune that puts the bees to sleep.

# Baby

Baby, a little precious creature born from its mother's womb.
Comes a sparkle of life.
The creator must be merciful to create such a beauty.
When I look into the eyes, I see a light, new life.
A little baby who entered the world, but the world is not ready for
     such greatness.
Lord, do not let this baby get caught in a swirl.
Let this child know beauty is found within.
For this beauty is great.
For it is gorgeous as a sunflower that shines in May.
And as strong as a lion in August.
For this baby is the new Mufusa crowned to be something marvelous.

# Good Day

Good day. I fancy you're filled with gloom.
When I see you, a rather pink butterfly flies through with tears in its
    eyes.
Ma'am, for why does it pour in July?
For such beautiful creatures to be born in the night.
Beast and beauties run all throughout this land.
I fancy I chose to be the beauty.
I am rather fine, don't you think?
For I can become anything I want to be.
It's a marvelous day; the birds sing if you just listen.
There is no mother nature.
It is just God's creation.
God created space that is not nature.
I fancy it is a good day a time to smile.
Forget the wolfs; they will soon find hope.
Just be you; understand what is all around you.
Not cars, TV, phone, or even humans.
Look at the grass and hear the breeze.
Sit and listen to everything from society turn off.
If you listen long enough in peace, God will speak.
Good day to all who hear the sounds of peace.

# Wife

I speak of gender, not a race.
Why can't men be strong to see a woman's gift?
Yes, we can be rather strong, but please open your eyes to the reward.
For what is a man without a woman?
Not many just one.
Is it that hard to simply erase flesh that will soon be filled with scars?
Can't you see there's many fish in the sea.
Good and bad, but I reckon no one is perfect.
For what is a woman without love.
Now this is meant to open your eyes to a woman's gift.
Not to tear down the man I want you to see.
Why God created Adam and Eve.
They stood by each other.
A wife knows how to bring life.
A wife knows how to nurse life and make it grow.
A wife knows how to teach in the word of peace.
A wife knows how to mend her family back together.
A wife knows the cost of beauty is not to be nasty but classy.
A wife knows how to hold a man when he is weak.
Realize the truth of a woman, a real woman
Who knows how to unlock these gifts.
For why do females walk this earth?

# Unlearned Father

Father, aren't you supposed to protect me?
For when you left my mother, you left me.
Why must you be so weak?
It is all connected; I keep running back to you.
Only for you to be worthless; you say you are sorry.
But keep eating me alive.
Am I speaking to a demon or the creator of all lies?
My heart was broken, busted by your neglect.
How could you want me some days, but not the other days?
You are confused, can't you see?
I tried to get you to open your eyes.
For a woman, you have chosen over me.
Can't you see I respected you? I forgave you.
And you wonder why Mother's Day is a bigger holiday.
For maybe they care about their child or children.
More than just burry a seed.
From flesh and leave it forgotten.
I cannot make you change only someone higher than me.
Higher than humanity, but then I am not sure if you could escape.
This hurt this pain, but I forgive you.
And I build you up because you are my father.
You were that hurt little boy who just grew up.
I know you can change and become God's best.
Far from great, but you are not the worst.
You gave me life; you gave me my fight.
You gave me strength through pain, and I honor you.
You gave me a reason to forgive, and I do it 1,000 times.
I will remember you, father, just a little boy with a lost fate.
Now it's time to follow Christ and become a man.
You had two children, but you gave it your unlearned best.
My unlearned father, I thank you from the bottom of my heart.

You gave me my war cry; I am in this world, but I am not immune
to evil.
Because of you, I found the greatest gift I found Christ.
There is no pain-free life; I cannot hide from the grief deep inside.
You created that flower to bloom into sunshine.
Sometimes I cannot stand the cry so Jesus walks by my side.
In fear of abuse, I found Christ who created my destiny.
I love you, I forgive you, and I cherish you,
My unlearned father!

# A Sign

Dream thunder clouds are rolling, awfully fast laid before me.

Is the ocean more like the aquarium?

My father and I are walking in excitement to see these great aquatic animals.

But at the bottom lays the demons.

The killers as if they were possessed.

Ready to kill great white sharks and killer whales and more.

Fear hit the bridge broke.

We fell in I rushed to the top.

I grabbed my father's hand the creatures were taking pieces of his flesh.

I screamed "Jesus!" the thunder lighting hit the water.

The aquatic animals were burnt alive.

Floating to the surface my father survived, but unfortunately, my prayers were the only thing keeping him alive.

# Fairy Tale

A little Black girl with wings takes flight high in the sky.
Other fairies are in the clouds having cherries.
Fairy is a sweet kind. But man can't seem to get along.
Perfect relationships are but a simple fairy tale.
Some in a love story that does not exist.
Everybody has challenges.
Like beauty and the beast but their love seems like a dream.
Only thing that binds a relationship together is the love of God.
True love is indeed not a fairy tale.
The love of God stands the test of time.
The love of Jesus is not a fairy tale put into a myth.

# Mustang

Such a beautiful horse and should not be tamed,
They live free not bothering anyone.
Every horse is not meant to ride; they must find a connection with
    their rider deep inside.
Attitude and sass, that's them.
Who does not like a horse with a little personality?
Beautiful species just living free.
Untouched, unbothered as they should.
Freedom runs their minds.
Their legs gallop riding into the wind.
As a herd, they are one.

# As a Wonder

Italy and France, I have been.
The beautiful gardens in France.
The music in Italy.
Both are great the boats traveling through the water.
Into the unknown or dancing salsa in front of a crowd cheering you
   on.
Or simply embracing your spirit.
Great food filled with love, what a design.
A masterpiece, a memory to keep.
As I dance stomping my feet, I create chemistry.
Radioactivity is everywhere; I feel the beat flow inside me.
My partner in quite amazement the way that I move.
The way my hips glide and my arms flow.
The smell of pasta and the people clapping.
In worldwide competition, I am the head, not the tail.
Unfortunately, it was just a dream.

# Not Satisfied

I am so sick of living a simple life stuck inside a box of untruth.
Cannot be happy for over two minutes.
I want to be happy forever.
My head hurts; my eyes are watering all because I am not satisfied.
I go to an event and leave with hurt because it did not last.
I do not need memories; I want dreams.
My brain is overloading with a need to get away.
To have friends who make a difference.
Yet I sit here in disbelief not wanting to dream.
I just want to go away from the hatred of man.
Because the people I needed the most were not there.
They sit as fools played by their own untruth.
Anger fills my heart, and no simple button to press to let it out.
My mood changes like time.
I just want a purposeful life that's not so boring.
I crave and crave more every time the sun rises and hurt fills my days
      when it falls.
I need more than me so I can soar.

# Grace

Grace is but a simple element.
For what will I have without grace.
Some say you are lucky, but I say favor is not fair.
For grace is powerful, some of us would be dead
Without grace a second chance.
For man must learn to live life not by the flesh but by the heart.
For when we decide to live by the flesh,
God still gives grace which I found is a great blessing.
You are but a seed, but you are depending on grace.
Water to pour and the sun to shine.
Therefore, you can bloom and rise.
Grace is the honor of benefaction.

# Trouble

Trouble is on your trail.
Running, looking for an exit.
Oh, what a rich man a poor man would do when he is in trouble.
Such power is held a fear rides your body.
Scared and afraid, therefore, you run, jump, and slide.
Just to reach the finish line.
Try to live life right because the death demon or angel is knocking
    at your door.
Waiting for you to breathe that last breath.
You run to the highest mountain just to escape fear and trouble.
Some fear water, heights, or spiders.
You began to lose your mind.
When trouble is knocking at your door, who will you run to?

# The Man with Desire

A man walks through a field of grass,
Lustful and greedy searching for someone or something to keep him
  satisfied.
And he was built and had some glory.
Just needed a beautiful woman to hold him.
For a man needs to be held to.
He goes all over the world searching for this woman.
This woman won't come easy as if she knows his motives.
For from man, she's learned to protect herself.
He walks with lust trying to get her.
Then she said until you become my lion king, your hair and body do
  not impress me.
I look at the soul.
He was used to women flocking to him.
He was saddened for once in his life.
He came back with honesty and honor.
A royal crown I do not desire.
For I am desperate for a woman with a pure heart.
To hold me for all my days.
For I will wait for your embrace.
The woman falls in love.
Therefore, she lists her terms, but she is strong but not perfect.
The man waits; they dance, they eat, but they do not sleep.
One day the man purposes to the woman. She says yes; they marry.
  Then they sleep in peace.

# Knowledge Is Power

The upper-class man builds up the cities he lives in but with a plan, a catch.
The Caucasian man builds up my city, only to include the upper class.
It seems that the middle class and lower class
Cannot dine in the prices of luxury are too high.
Most consider themselves middle class, but it seems the middle is encountering the lower.
The rich man has knowledge to indirectly push out the lower man.
Knowledge is power, leverage over the weak-minded.
The White, Black, Asian, and Hispanic, these races fight each other.
Mostly just the White man against the colored man including all people of color, not just Black.
This can also be assumptions to cause chaos or confusion.
For all Black men are not ghetto or poor.
All White men do not think they are superior.
All Asian do not practice martial arts.
We must come together as a unit.
For the White man might deliver a cuisine only for the upper-class man to enjoy.
But the knowledge the Black man must receive and build.
To work together they can conquer the next.
The ignorant man is useless.
Knowledge is power.

# Dark Side

I thought everybody had a dark side.
Flesh that just was suppressed by discipline.
I was foolish and ignorant to think that flesh was just negative.
But I realized it was positive if applied in the right way.
At one point I thought everybody was nice and sweet.
Reality hits; trials and tribulations hit.
The dark side only comes out when the devil holds you tight.
When fear, anger, revenge, lust, greed, selfishness, and envy
Build up inside which makes the heart turn cold.
I realized the dark side is when your hurt and you spread hurt.
When you smile to keep from crying.
When you wear a mask because of reality.
Personal life enters a storm you carry the load.
Why carry stress and abuse?
Why not let it go?
Childhood abuse or simply how you were raised built up this dark
    side.
Jesus is a savior who will hold you in the mist of life's storm.
It is okay to be broken, ashamed, and abused.
Mental or physical, God mends all.
You must heal if you want peace within yourself.
Stop running from the savior Christ; just choose to move forward.
Stop running from the truth only; it will set you free.
If you keep running, darkness clouds your days.

# Beale Street

I was on a field trip.
Had no idea of a future, lost between friends, only had God.
Women and men in time change.
I was on a school field trip walking downtown, just left the civil
   rights museum.
Learning history with a talent for dance.
It was my school's field trip.
The girls were envious and full of jealousy and hated my talent.
Yet I moved forward.
A woman, my dance teacher, saw my talent but refused to let it shine.
I always connected with adults more than children.
This man was singing on Beale Street and had to pass him for lunch
   at some diner.
He kept singing in a white suit and shoes.
I forgot how much I loved music blues, an old sweet sound.
I joined him in shock and danced with him.
He helped me, this 100-year-old man.
The other girls did not see and are kind of jealous.
My teacher telling me to join the group, but I couldn't because I had
   to say, "Thank you."
This one-hundred-year-old man was lost in happiness of the blues
   and simply jazz.
As I danced to the saxophone.
We needed each other to spread some comfort and happiness.
The man helped me when my dance team did not see me.
We understood time and each other, the gift of jazz.

# Fashion

Some say I can wear anything I look good.
Let's be honest, when you look good, you feel good.
A common statement but true.
You can wear something ugly, but you think it is cute, so you feel
  cute.
But constructive criticism you must take.
Hate you do not.
The truth can hurt, but you must know the difference.
But fashion can be great funny, ugly, or cute.
Whichever you prefer, for me I choose cute.
Fashion only lasts a while.
Style lasts for generations.
It creates a purpose and image.

# Heart

The heart can be pure or evil.
You can look at a pure heart.
The person can be ugly on the outside, but the natural eye becomes
    tricked by the spiritual eye.
To only see beauty on the outside.
Because of the heart, you fall in love.
The heart is surrounded by veins which can become silver and shine
    bright.
Light always has a way to creep through the darkness.
The heart is the center of the body, but a powerful thing in the nat-
    ural and spiritual.

# Prayer

What is a prayer? Is it simply a conversation
You have with the Lord?
You create a relationship because without a relationship,
Favor and anointing are left out.
A prayer simply shows you having a talk getting deep and personal.
With God creating a personal relationship where you can grow and
      find life, miracles, and solutions,
Prayer can be a powerful weapon if you create a relationship.
Do not take the gift of prayer easily,
For it is a sweet victory.
When you cry, God feels.
When you rejoice, God is glorified.
His beloved son, Jesus, did not die just to rise again.
He died that the Lord might answer a sinner's prayer.

# Imperfect the Inner Circle

I wish I could trust a man like I do God, but I am imperfect just like
the next man.

I look at my inner circle which is small.

The men and women in the circle I question the trust.

I look to my mother; she's private and unsure.

I look to my father; I can't tell simple accomplishments because of
envy.

They look to me, the people I love, they start to question.

My haters look some seen some not.

I lie awake in a fifteen-year-old's mind as my soul escapes.

I have made mistakes unsure of my choices.

So, I wait, I cry a simple prayer for escape.

The coward dies; the strong survives, but what is the price to pay?

Keep fighting day and night for peace.

The fear of the unknown man crumbles at its embrace.

I choose faith to step out and hope I won't fall.

To run through the storm, to hope there is another side.

To claim the name Jesus and refuse Satan's flag.

For why should I vouch for evil or simply not listen just to be swal-
lowed in my own deception of sin?

Why not choose the clouds or the pure and kind?

For what I want the imperfect to realize that deception is in the inner
circle I cry.

I want love, peace, and trust in my inner circle for every imperfect
man's lies.

# Golden Heart

A heart that is golden but covered in winter's ice.
Filled with a lover's romance and quite the thrill.
The golden heart beats slower and slower as the ice thickens.
Here comes a nail with love to break the ice.
The cracks spread; the ice wants to hold the heart's cry.
The heart is pure but blinded by the unseen realm
Of defeat, and fear breaks through, but the heart still beats.
There is hope for a future of love and kindness.

# Older Woman

The wife guilts the shame of her reproduction.
Bullied by man being the boss but angels.
Watch them fly in the womb and in the hearts of women.
The unseen hand of God pulls the younger women in their paths.
They're supposed to be mentors; they give gifts.
Unsure of how to say, "I care about you."
They need and want to realize the golden star that creates.
When the younger meets the older.
Let the wisdom intersect with the questions of life's roots.
The race and culture do not matter, just the walk of love.
The walk of love is to look past the offense.
Selfishness and pride lead to a dead end.
But love shows care for others rather than yourself.

# Hindrance in the Worry of Love

I love my son and my daughter, but I create a shield.
Because they are a part of me, no one else.
I hold them in my heart; I worry, so I overprotect.
Place my daughter in a wheelchair.
My son is the follower, not head.
My daughter runs and can even walk.
My son has the strength of a true man.
I see, but I am blinded by the false.
If the man I love will tell me the truth.
My spouse cannot see the worry.
For if the head stinks, the whole body does.
God said, "Set them free"; he had to send me a man
To tell me the raw truth.
I let my daughter walk and placed discipline.
I let my son take the head and be the leader.
I passed the gift of sincere faith, and I left stress-free.

# Bullied

Bullied into the eyes of man, I cannot breathe.
The other is the one with no opinion.
Grow, men and women and the young.
When does it end the lonely the fear?
I want to fight back, but I cannot scream.
Tears roll down my face of the feared.
Did I choose life or death?
The sacred place or the place of freedom.
I refuse to be strapped by man and their sin.
I refuse not to be a woman of strength.
I roar like thunder, they crash not me.
I am running to that victory; man places me in a handicap.
But Jesus gives me his Holy Spirit.
No matter how I was born early or late.
God said that I am greatness, so I break loose.
Like an earthquake to shatter the enemy, not man.
For I realized who I love—myself, family, friends, teachers, and the
    unwise man.
But I dare not to be a fool to the foolish and unwise.
They don't know me; only God does.
Hear me roar!

# Angels

Guard me, hold me, wrap me in your wings.
Don't let go; don't leave me here in this place.
Take me to the heavenly places where I dream of love.
All I see are tears and demons around me.
The classmates, coworkers, adults, and children.
Spirits have no age, no color, no signs.
Angels I need to fight in my body and spirit.
I cannot deal with my personal problems.
I bring to work to my children!
I need angels!
Like the earth needs the sun.
Like my body needs the holy spirit.
I need angels!
Forget the man; forget my husband.
Forget my mother, my father!
I need supernatural power.
Something to fight the unseen!
I need the angels!

# The Thought Process of the Broken Man!

I don't need love from my husband or wife.
I don't need another prayer from someone I love.
There is a thin line between love and hate.
Between friendship and use.
I don't need assurance of a man.
Or validation from my students.
Or a letter that says, "I love you. I look up to you."
I don't need laying on of hands.
I need the one I love back.
I cannot seem to move forward.
I'm supposed to be my old self.
Friendship broke, and I see it every day.
I need you!
I need Jesus!
I need God!
I need a sign!
I need a home!
I need some direction on the roles I play.
I am blinded, says my mother.
But she cannot see the pain.
Or begin to understand the dedication, motivation, the education.
I need you!

# I Believe in Love Again!

I believe in the love of Adam and Eve.
I believe in the love of a man and a woman.
And the way a man holds a woman in his arms of protection.
The way a woman takes care of the man's needs.
I believe in miracles that love can last forever.
I believe in marriage and sacred love.
I am the guitar; he is the singer who brings me to life.
We're in the Amazon of reality of color of love.
I believe in the angels who dance when we kiss.
As a holy place of spirit.
I believe in young and old love.
The White, Black, and biracial love.
I believe in slow dances and holding each other.
I believe in smiles and laughter.
I know that a couple's love will not fail.
If God is put first, love will rise like the wind.

# Two Best Friends from Different Decades!

A young girl with a pure heart,
A mother with a pure heart
Meet each other on summer's day.
Love and peace fill their relationship.
They both cherish the relationship created in God's eyes
No matter the age
Or the difference in roles they play.
They found each other, and the little girl was grateful
For this woman's wisdom and kindness.
And yet it started from a prayer.
A sweet word from a young girl to a beautiful lady.
They needed each other more than they realized.
For if they separate or fall apart, heaven would cry.
For the power of their friendship shakes demons and hell.
The mascot might be the devil, but a spirit meets a spirit.
For men and women do not understand the spirit of kindness.
For the power of friendship is powerful.
And I choose to cherish it!

# Passion, Lies

What is passion, what is happiness?
My dreams have flustered away into thin air.
My dream of a family and a spouse.
Seem too far to catch often on edge.
I want happiness a job I love.
I am quite sick of people, but yet them I love.
I want to help young men be strong.
I want to help society grow in strength.
I also want money to leave for my children and their children.
Fire of the Holy Ghost hit for every passion lies.
Purify my heart, my mind, my soul that is so blind.
My tears fall, and they burn into sweet victory.
Cleanse my heart, every single vain.
Tired and ashamed of my life's plan.
Give me a vision, a dream, open thy eyes to see.
Forget them; remember me.
My passion is lost and cannot be found.
I need the fire to awaken it, burn the glass.
And open the case of my destiny.
Holy Ghost prevails fire fall.
This poor sinner soul cries.
For I am your servant.
Holy is the name of Jesus where the fire is released.

# Perception of Sin

The human race is really confused off perception.
What they see is really the truth.
They turn blind eyes to pain.
They sit and laugh at destruction because what they see is production.
There blinded by their mistakes, so they fear the truth.
The way you look at things creates the product.
The perception of the eyes.
The natural is just a perception.
The spiritual is being awakened.
Why can't you see an attack before it happens that creates the
    perception?
You sit in authority over children as a teacher.
As a mentor or even as a pastor.
Yet your perception is not the truth it is lies.
Sin that clouds your judgment.
You cannot help a child or student if your perception is unclear.
It's best to remove and stay home.
When a student walks through your door, they expect to be intrigued.
Maybe forget the pain, for in pain, there is motivation.
They do not expect you to raise them, only to teach them.
If you know that their parents have little common sense.
Why turn a blind eye? Is it because your story is weak-minded?
The way you look at life the truth will create your perception.

# Deception of Sin

When you deceive, that creates deception; it creates sin.
Deception is very much a sin as any other sin.
You hide your hand.
You stab.
You forget.
You turn a blind eye.
You leave your children.
You disrespect your elders.
Racism
Pride
All of these things create deception.
The hard part is when you cannot see the deception.
Sin has clouded your vision.
If you find yourself guilty of any of these things.
Look in the mirror, face the demon, and stop running.
God has promised us all forgiveness; no sin is too much for him.
Stress, sorrow, abuse, neglect, rejection.
Now these are emotions also feelings.
But they too create deception; they deceive a woman or man.
Whenever you feel empty, something seems to be missing,
Look deep inside the soul, and you will find the answer.
God gives every man a choice running is deception.
Therefore, if God gives freedom, why must you deceive yourself?
Forgive me for my eyes are small.
Forgive me for my eyes are blind.
And my vision was blurry.
My fears cause trouble.
This is my deception of sin.

# Insight on Reality

Vision is so important to see clearly.
Sin blocks out the reality.
Life is a lesson; humans are imperfect.
Choices are given; mistakes are made.
Just because we have insight does not make it a reality.
Right is right if you find yourself in a hole.
You have lost sight of reality.
A follower
The popular kid
The joker
A hypocrite
All these words mean nothing without the man who holds them.
When you claim you're a Christian, but everything you do is against
    the Word.
Why not just be you? Is it because when you get scared, in trouble,
    you find God?
Why use the name Jesus but not obey the rules?
Do rules and structure matter anymore?
If we did not have the law, would we be safe?
If God did not place rules, we would be lost.
If you know the answer to this question,
Please step outside the tricks of the enemy.
And step into reality of what's around you.

# Erotic Love

Now this love is misused and abused.
*Love* is just a complex word when thoughts and sin
Get ahold of it; erotic love, how sweet,
How desired; there is nothing wrong with desiring this sweet love.
But this love has a limit, let's be honest.
God created an erotic love of romance between husband and wife.
Marriage, but it is often used just in relationship.
There are no boundaries; this love is a privilege.
This love used in the wrong action can be a curse.
Why do so many bad things come from sex, if it is love?
See when used in the wrong position, now Satan has authority
To create confusion; think about it now.
My friends, young people, listen, discipline is strength.
It is the strength of saying, "I fought the desire, and I waited."
There is a future that lies ahead; no, tomorrow is not promised.
But if you live for today and find strength, tomorrow will come.
God promised us life; there is no need for us in heaven.
So why did he build the earth?
Remember there is nothing wrong with erotic love.
But when you use it, use it in the positive direction.
For this love springs life and joy.

# Dishonest Man

I dislike the man who smiles in your face.
And then spreads lies of gossip.
Or the man who throws the rock but hides his hand.
For this is a coward, for that is truth.
The man or woman who runs and hides,
When they encounter a sweet spirit or a kind person,
They become tense, wait for the right moment to strike.
I dislike the man who says, "I support you, sending you up in prayer."
Then you are fighting extra demons.
Instead of being a woman or man enough to tell you
To your face.
The world does not need cowards or punks.
Men or women, we need strength and brave.
For if children raise children, you get the last days.

# Life

My friends, my foes, please, I beg you to remember life.
Life is important; life is everything.
God does not need us.
For he created the earth, the sea, and all that is in it.
Revenge never ends with two shots and one blow.
And yet the pain is still there.
What story is this? What life is this?
Do not die early because of ignorance.
People perish through a lack of knowledge.
Listen, for once, look deep.
Do not speak words of negativity for they will come to pass.
Do not speak words into existence for the enemy hears all.
Life is so important, so valuable.
Love is the same, but life creates love.

# Christian Girl

If I look at the time
And I look at the clouds
That lies there on the noonday,
I see the hope of a Black girl
Waiting in the wasteland of all the bones.
They are dry, and there is no hope left.
Friends are few, and I see God come down.
And heal all that was lost.
I look at my ancestors, and the Black woman lay before me.
The woman who could smile, walk, and talk
In such a way that inspired a young girl like me.
So I kept walking with my head lifted up.
When the sun lays waste on my arms,
My Black arms, and my hands,
The wisdom of the soul leaves the earth.
But there I stand knowing one day I will see them again.
I hope all of them are happy and found a love that will last forever.
The love of God is the love I have as a Christian girl.
A Christian that I am, a Christian girl all that I know.
Yes, I know of flesh, and yes, I know of sin.
But I do not know the truth that lies within.
Because God can look at my heart and see the coils and the sharpens.
It's imperative that I can see it, but sometimes I don't.
And that's okay because God still loves me anyway.
Yes, I am that Christian, that rock hiding in the wind.
That free, that paper, that pen, that weakness.
That is the Christian girl that I am.
A Christian who is very misunderstood cannot be understood by the
        eyes of man.
I am that girl.
That girl who longs for the Lord to be glorified.

But yet I stand with my foundation unstable.
But yet I rise.
Because there is a hope that lies in the sky.
There's a hope that lies in my heart.
There's a hope I know so well.
There's a hope that's made me quiet, mute to live out the good life
of faith.
To not be so bold, to say it all the time.
But there's a hope as a Christian girl that I know which is Jesus.
And Jesus I find.
A Christian girl buried in her own heart.

# A Girl's Heart in the Darkness

I have not been a woman, but I have been a girl.
Grounded and buried in my own decisions in my own swirl.
I have felt the voices of adult conversation.
I watched the plague that my relatives,
that people who I known and loved placed.
And yet they say blood is thicker than water.
I have seen water to be thicker than wine.
I have seen the torn, and I have seen the tormented.
And my heart has been broken by the decisions
That ignorance has made.
And sometimes you think of it as stupidity.
Like how could you not see the common sense that lies in the
    situation.
But yet I think, did they even know common sense existed?
They have not been trained or thought to be trained.
In a profession, school is vastly needed because it trains the mind.
And it is a powerful thing; it is quite a unique machine.
It is a machine that cannot be held back
But pushed forward; the mind is so great,
But yet we as humans, cannot create a mind because our mind.
That was then created by a higher being.
Some have got the visions to see that face.
Some in the Bible, some in stories.
That got to see Jesus; they got to see his face.
Yet as young people, we are generations who do not see his face.
But we have his word, his word that is life.
That word might not be life to you; it might just be a simple lie.
Whatever it is to you, I suggest you think or rethink your steps.
And no, I am not judging you for who you want to be.

A Muslim, Jew, priest, and atheist.
Whatever it is that you want to be.
But I ask that you look deep.
Stop running from the hurt because in the hurt is where you truly
    see.
Look at the stories, and look at the hardness of the stories.
And remember as Christians, they were not simple.
They were not easily overplayed; they were hardened.
The only reason we survived was because there is a God who could
    heal them.
There was a God who stood with us.
And ceased the problems; this is the truth.
This is the life; this is what all we can see that lies in the pit.
The pit of darkness that can be so dark yet so open.
With just a match of light.

# Mindset

I am tired of being sick and tired.
I am going to make a difference.
I will stop caring about what negative people think of me.
I will please only God and no other man.
I deserve love and happiness.
It's time for fitness; it's time to check me.
I am a winner and victor.
I will survive, and I will have heaven here on earth.
When plan A does not work, I will keep pushing.
When plan B does not work, I will keep pushing.
I deserve happiness!
I loved my enemies; I forgave those who abandoned me.
I am still forgiving in spite of my pain.
I deserve freedom!

# Cleanse of the Body

The N-word, the B-word.
Such vulgar, such with foul play.
In hip-hop music, it lies culture.
But it is still poison, that poison that was used.
On my ancestors and today, we say it as if it is nothing.
I have condemned myself yet out of ignorance and stupidity.
I have said the words I have danced to the songs.
Listen to the beat which music can also be the defeat.
I lay there in the wasteland looking at these words.
And yet these words are fatal; they are poison,
No matter how you change it.
You can poison the man, and you can cremate him.
And put him in ashes, yet the poison still shows.
It never dies in any format or position that you put it in.
So why do we say it?
Some of us say because we are Black, we can say it.
But it is still a poison, a poison that tore down the Black man,
That tore down the Black woman; we as women are treated at its
    despise.
Hip-hop music, we are talked about; we are perceived as the B-words.
And dare not to spell it, because again,
I don't want to condemn myself.
For there are words laid in the power of the tongue.
Words you can speak into existence.
And words that can cause life-or-death situations.
So why not use our words wisely?
Because these words have kept us back.
That have held us back for so many generations.
The generations that have come and those in the future.
The words are in the tongue.

For the tongue to be such a small thing yet it is so powerful.
And yet if I am a Christian woman, and I say these words,
Then I am a hypocrite.

# A Closing Prayer for My Readers!

Lord, they have finished this book with victory and honor. Lord, have their hearts open and more focused on you. More than themselves, remove doubt and destruction from their lives. Let their mental health increase with the peace of God that surpasses all understanding. Patience to play every role that you placed in their lives. Freedom they carry every time they pray a prayer. You will answer for you said, "Knock, and the door shall be opened." Lord, hear their prayer for they are your children. They walk in the full authority of Christ Jesus; when they call your name, mountains move. Storms cease, and problems find their solutions. Lord, if they're in need of healing, release it, father. I pray a prayer of a saint called by your holy name (Heb. 3:1). I bless this reader, and I love them with the love of Christ. In Jesus's name, amen.

# Acknowledgments

I first give thanks, honor, and glory to God, my Father, for placing these gifts of the spirit in my life and for showing me my truth and blessing my life with family and wonderful people.

I want to thank my aunt for giving me the inspiration to write this book. I also want to thank my church family for supporting me!

Also, every other teacher, student, family, or friend who accepted prayer. I am so proud of my family and all the wonderful people who have touched my life. I love you all. May peace and growth rest in our relationships. Far and wide and most of all, I hope God shines through me with a laugh or prayer just when you need it!

# About the Author

I am Kayla Ross, a fifteen-year-old writer, the author of this book. What inspired me to write this book was to spread light and wisdom to all generations. This book is a book of poems to share with you not only the inner me, the visions that inspire me, but also the truth that builds me as a young lady. As a writer, this book is titled *Visions of My Heart*. These poems show dreams, visions, and experiences that I have had; some are based on true stories in my life. Off the dreams, I want to become reality. I really wanted to inspire my generation. I want them to see a young face on the cover of a book that they would want to pick it up and read about. I also have a message behind each poem that conveys wisdom. I learned that wisdom does not come through age but through experience. Faith is powerful to me, and this book is not just for Christians but also for the faint of heart. Therefore, I encourage you to read and think of the messages being conveyed. Learn the depth of the message and its story and the appreciation of the things and people around you that simply create you. Thank you so much for buying this book. I hope you genuinely enjoy it and learn something from it. I also pray that it will bless every area of your life! Thank you!